The Thrifty Parents' Guide to Arts & Crafts:
Bible Edition

by DeAnna Van De Brake

BIRCH BENCH PRESS

TASTY BOOKS

Van De Brake, DeAnna.
2nd edition.
ISBN: 978-1-938912-10-8

Interior Layout by Lea C. Deschenes
Cover Designed by Joshua Grieve
Author Photo by Derrick Brown
Illustrations by Jen Stemple
Edited by Derrick Brown and Hannah Safren

Special thanks to the generous support of Nancy Counts

Birch Bench Press

The Thrifty Parents' Guide to Arts & Crafts: Bible Edition!

PART ONE

BIBLE RELATED ACTIVITIES FOR PARENTS AND CHILDREN

CREATE SOMETHING NEW

DISCUSSION:

Explain to your kids that God is the creator of all things. Talk to them about how amazing it is that God made the earth, the sky, the animals, and all other living things. Let your kids know that God gave them their own ability to invent, and now they are going to make their own creations.

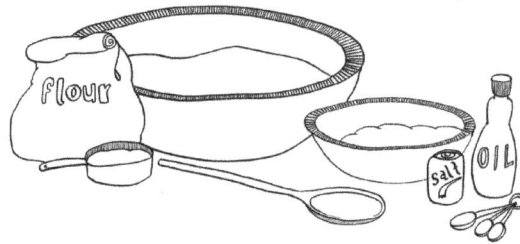

SUPPLIES:
➢ Homemade play-dough

Items needed

➢ 2 cups flour
➢ 1 cup of salt
➢ 2 tbsp cream of tartar
➢ 2 tbsp of oil
➢ Food coloring,
➢ (Optional) Cinnamon or peppermint extract for fragrance
➢ 3 bowls

Directions

> - Mix 2 cups flour and 1 cup salt into one bowl
> - Mix 2 tbsp of cream of tartar and 2 tbsp of oil into a separate bowl, then stir.
> - Combine all of the ingredients into a bowl and stir.
> - Heat slowly in a skillet until dough begins to pull together and away from the edge of pan.
> - Add food coloring to dye the dough, and cinnamon or peppermint extract for fragrance (Optional)
> - Remove the now-colored dough from the skillet and place it on a countertop.
>   May want to cover the countertops for an easy clean.
> - Knead the dough
> - Store in a zip-lock bag until ready to use.

ACTIVITY:

> - Give the kids the dough and allow them to create something new.
> - Provide examples: Maybe a monkey with big duck feet? Or a giraffe with wings?
> - Have the kids name their new creation.

REVIEW VERSE: Genesis 1:1

1 *In the beginning God created the heavens and the earth*

② SAFARI

DISCUSSION:

Explain that at the beginning it was only Adam, but God knew that Adam would be lonely so God made animals for Adam to name and enjoy. Have a discussion about respecting animals. Tell them that the combination of all the species included is what makes the earth so wonderful.

SUPPLIES:

➢   All the stuffed animals that you can find

ACTIVITY:

➢   Disperse the animals throughout the playing area
➢   Tell the kids that you are going on a Safari to find and name all of the animals, just as Adam once did.
➢   Tour the house together and when an animal is spotted, have your kid name the animal and the noise it makes.

REVIEW VERSE: Genesis 2:18-20

18 And the LORD God said, "It is not good that man should be alone; I will make him a helper comparable to him." 19 Out of the ground the LORD God formed every beast of the field and every bird of the air, and brought them to Adam to see what he would call them. And whatever Adam called each living creature, that was its name.

③

HIDE AND SEEK

DISCUSSION:
God is always pursuing us because he wants a close relationship with us. Explain to them that God is everywhere and even when we are hiding or lost, God is near.

SUPPLIES:
➤ Just yourselves and a safe place to hide and seek

ACTIVITY:
➤ Have one person be the "Seeker" (God). Tell the other kids to be the "Hiders" (Adam or Eve).
➤ Have the Seeker count to 30 while everyone else hides within the designated playing area.
➤ When the Seeker finishes counting, have he/she search for those in hiding.

REVIEW VERSE: Genesis 3:8
8 And they heard the sound of the LORD God walking in the garden in the cool of the day, and Adam and his wife hid themselves from the presence of the LORD God among the trees of the garden.

4

BUILD-A-BOAT

DISCUSSION:
Talk about Noah's Ark, the great flood, and why Noah only brought a certain amount of animals with him. Let your kids know that God believes in us and after the flood, He helped Noah rebirth the earth for future generations.

SUPPLIES:
- Big poster paper
- Construction paper (computer paper works to)
- Scissors
- Crayons
- Tape

ACTIVITY:
- Have the kids use these crayons to draw a big boat, just like Noah's Ark, on the poster board,
- Use the construction paper to draw and color as many animals as they want.
- Cut out the animals and tape them onto boat

REVIEW VERSE: Genesis 7:2-4
2 You shall take with you seven each of every clean animal, a male and his female; two each of animals that are unclean, a male and his female; 3 also seven each of birds of the air, male and female, to keep the species alive on the face of all the earth. 4 For after seven more days I will cause it to rain on the earth forty days and forty nights, and I will destroy from the face of the earth all living things that I have made."

5

TUMBLING TOWER

DISCUSSION:
Remember that even the things humans can build, make, and think of, are gifts from God. He gives us the power and intelligence to do a lot of cool things!

SUPPLIES:
➢ Legos, blocks or dominoes

ACTIVITY:
➢ See who can build the highest tower before it falls.
➢ If there aren't enough supplies, take turns building or build the tower together

REVIEW VERSE: Genesis 11:4-7
4 And they said, "Come, let us build ourselves a city, and a tower whose top is in the heavens; let us make a name for ourselves, lest we be scattered abroad over the face of the whole earth." 5 But the LORD came down to see the city and the tower which the sons of men had built. 6 And the LORD said, "Indeed the people are one and they all have one language, and this is what they begin to do; now nothing that they propose to do will be withheld from them. 7 Come, let Us go down and there confuse their language, that they may not understand one another's speech."

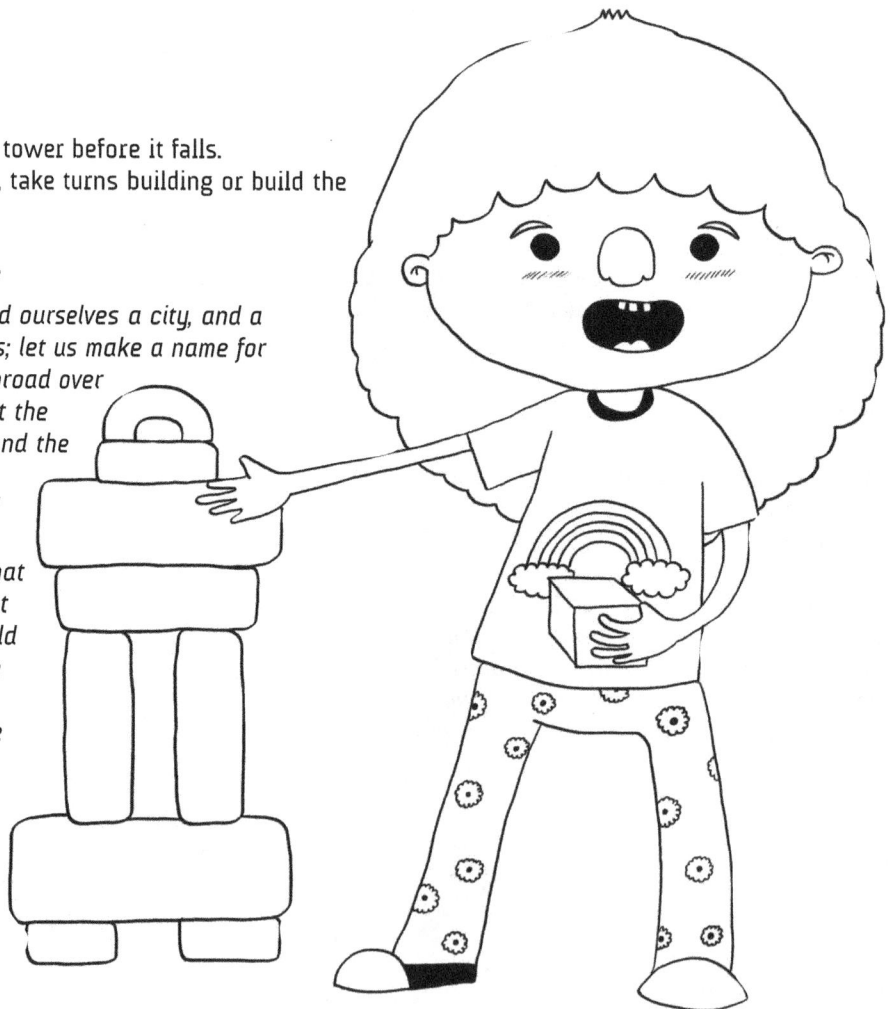

6

POP A COMPLIMENT

DISCUSSION:
God loves to bless us. When we pay attention, we can see His beautiful gifts everywhere. Tell your kids that the air we breathe, the trees we climb and the flowers we pick are just a few of God's many blessings. It is good to thank Him and to thank people who help you.

SUPPLIES:
➢ Balloons
➢ Paper
➢ Writing utensil

ACTIVITY:
➢ Give everyone participating a scrap piece of paper, a pencil and a balloon.
➢ Everyone writes something nice on his/her sheet of paper.
➢ After they are finished, they should put the paper inside the balloon and then blow up the balloon.
➢ Hand each person a different balloon
➢ Let each person pop their balloon and read off their message before the next person goes.

REVIEW VERSE: Genesis 21:1-3
The Lord said unto Abram... I will bless thee...

7

SPLIT DESSERT

DISCUSSION:

Talk to your kids about the importance of sharing. Explain that if we are greedy and keep things to ourselves, we will pay the consequences of having few or no friends, an empty heart, and unhappiness. If we give and share we will, in return, be given to and shared with and have a rad heart!

SUPPLIES:
- ➤ A bag of any treats; EX. M&M's or a plate of strawberries. Something that all the children enjoy.
- ➤ Paper
- ➤ Pencil
- ➤ Bucket/ hat
- ➤ Plastic zip lock bags

ACTIVITY:
- ➤ The parents lay out a pile of candy or treats, making some piles larger than others (reserve some goodies where the kids can't see it.)
- ➤ Kids pretend to be Abraham and let Mom and Dad choose first.
- ➤ Parents choose the best and most like Lot did.
- ➤ Kids get the "leftovers".
- ➤ Parents say "Surprise!" and then pull out the reserved goodies and give the children twice as much as the parents received because they weren't selfish!

REVIEW VERSE: Genesis 13:8 (NIV)

Lets not have any quarreling between you and me..." Abraham let Lot choose first.

8

SEA TAG

DISCUSSION:
The Lord is our protector. Talk to your kids about how He protected the Israelites on their escape from Egypt. Name some other ways He has protected you and your family.

SUPPLIES:
➢ An open area to play
➢ Something to mark where the "river" begins.

ACTIVITY:
➢ Get a blue blanket or towel for the ocean.
➢ The kids start on the edge of the blanket or make a 10 foot "Red Sea" with tape.
➢ Parents start about 20 feet away from the kids.
➢ Say go!
➢ Kids run across the Sea to the other side.
➢ Parents chase kids (Egyptians chase the Israelites).
➢ Once the kids are on the other side, they are safe.
➢ Parents have to try to tag them, but if they touch the water they must pretend to drown

REVIEW VERSE: Exodus 14:15,16,
15 And the LORD said to Moses, "Why do you cry to Me? Tell the children of Israel to go forward. 16 But lift up your rod, and stretch out your hand over the sea and divide it. And the children of Israel shall go on dry ground through the midst of the sea.

9

DRAWING COMMANDMENTS

DISCUSSION:
The Ten Commandments are the fundamentals of God's teachings. Talk your kids through the Ten Commandments and tell them what each one means and why they are important. Together you will draw pictures to help remember the commandments.

SUPPLIES:
➢ Paper
➢ Pencil
➢ Crayons

ACTIVITY:
➢ Write one commandment per piece of paper.
➢ Divvy out one or two commandments based on how many people are participating.
➢ Each person should draw a picture to represent the commandments they were given.
➢ Talk through why each person chose to draw what they did. Be creative!

REVIEW VERSE: Exodus 20: 3-17
3 "You shall have no other gods before Me. 4 You shall not make for yourself a carved image—any likeness of anything that is in heaven above, or that is in the earth beneath, or that is in the water under the earth; 5 you shall not bow down to them nor serve them. For I, the LORD your God, am a jealous God, visiting the iniquity of the fathers upon the children to the third and fourth generations of those who hate Me, 6 but showing mercy to thousands, to those who love Me and keep My commandments. 7 You shall not take the name of the LORD your God in vain, for the LORD will not hold him guiltless who takes His name in vain. 8 Remember the Sabbath day, to keep it holy. 9 Six days you shall labor and do all your work, 10 but the seventh day is the Sabbath of the LORD your God. In it you shall do no work: you, nor your son, nor your daughter, nor your male servant, nor your female servant, nor your cattle, nor your stranger who is within your gates.11 For in six days the LORD made the heavens and the earth, the sea, and all that is in them, and rested the seventh day. Therefore the LORD blessed the Sabbath day and hallowed it. 12 Honor your father and your mother, that your days may be long upon the land which the LORD your God is giving you. 13 You shall not murder. 14 You shall not commit adultery. 15 You shall not steal. 16 You shall not bear false witness against your neighbor. 17 You shall not covet your neighbor's house; you shall not covet your neighbor's wife, nor his male servant, nor his female servant, nor his ox, nor his donkey, nor anything that is your neighbor's."

(10)

BLOW THE TRUMPET!

DISCUSSION:
God is a mighty warrior – awesome in power. Talk about how He will lead us in the right direction for the right reasons, we just need to trust in Him.

SUPPLIES:
➤ Blocks
➤ Small ball
➤ Safe open area
➤ Horn

ACTIVITY:
➤ Build a tower of blocks
➤ Stand 5, 10 or 15 feet from the block building (dependent on age/strength of person throwing)
➤ Blow the horn
➤ Use the ball and try and knock down the block building

REVIEW VERSE: Joshua 6: 4-5
4 And seven priests shall bear seven trumpets of rams' horns before the ark. But the seventh day you shall march around the city seven times, and the priests shall blow the trumpets. 5 It shall come to pass, when they make a long blast with the ram's horn, and when you hear the sound of the trumpet, that all the people shall shout with a great shout; then the wall of the city will fall down flat. And the people shall go up every man straight before him."

11

ROYALTY FOR THE HOUR

DISCUSSION:
Talk to your kids about Saul. Mention how He was King and forgot to put God first. Tell them that sometimes power can make you forget that God is the most powerful of all and we cannot forget to love Him most. Tell your kids that they will each get the opportunity to be in charge.

SUPPLIES:
- Paper
- Crayons
- Tape

ACTIVITY:
- Tape two sheets of paper together horizontally.
- Decorate the sheets of paper with crayons
- Cut the top of the paper in waves or triangles (optional)
- Tape the ends of the paper together to complete a circular shape.
- Place the crown on the King or Queen of the hour
- Allow the King or Queen to be in charge for the hour. Depending on the time of the day, they can choose what to eat for lunch, or what board game to play.

REVIEW VERSE: 1 Samuel 10:23, 24
23 So they ran and brought him from there; and when he stood among the people, he was taller than any of the people from his shoulders upward. 24 And Samuel said to all the people, "Do you see him whom the LORD has chosen, that there is no one like him among all the people?" So all the people shouted and said "Long live the King."

12

DECORATE CARDS

DISCUSSION:
God is always looking at the beauty on the inside of us. It doesn't matter how we look on the outside, God loves us all the same.

SUPPLIES:
➢ Construction paper
➢ Crayons
➢ Any spare craft items
➢ Glue

ACTIVITY:
➢ Fold the construction paper horizontally
➢ Leave the outside of the card blank and have each child color the inside of the card with everything and anything they like.

REVIEW VERSE: 1 Samuel 16:7
7 But the LORD said to Samuel, "Do not look at his appearance or at his physical stature, because I have refused him. For the LORD does not see as man sees; for man looks at the outward appearance, but the LORD looks at the heart."

(13)

SLINGSHOT

DISCUSSION:
David and Goliath is a story of one man having faith and confidence. Talk about how David defeated Goliath, even though he was so much smaller. Talk about how confidence or trust in God can lead to great things.

SUPPLIES:
- Newspaper
- Tape
- Rubber-bands
- Ping-pong ball
- Empty can
- Safe open area

ACTIVITY:

Create the slingshot
- Grab three sheets of newspaper and roll them together very tightly, until it resembles a long pole.
- Wrap tape around the pole of newspaper, to make it very sturdy.
- Bend it, so it resemble a "V"
- Tie two rubber-bands together, so that one loop can go over one side of the "V" and the other loop can go over the other side of the "V"

Rules
- Once the slingshot is completed, place a ping-pong ball in the center of the rubber bands and pull it back with one hand, while holding the bottom of the "V" with the other hand.
- Place a can on top of something high and pretend that the can is the face of Goliath.
- Have the kids try to shoot the can down.

REVIEW VERSE: 1 Samuel 17: 23, 24
23 Then as he talked with them, there was the champion, the Philistine of Gath, Goliath by name, coming up from the armies of the Philistines; and he spoke according to the same words. So David heard them. 24 And all the men of Israel, when they saw the man, fled from him and were dreadfully afraid.

FRIENDSHIP BRACELETS

DISCUSSION:
Lots of folks are too nervous to tell others how cool they are, how funny or pretty they are. Saying nice things out loud is a great way to spark a friendship. Talk about friendship and how important it is to let people know that they are cared about.

SUPPLIES:
➢ String
➢ Fruit-loops Cereal

ACTIVITY:
➢ Put fruit-loops on a string,
➢ Have the kids help each other tie the bracelets around their wrists.

REVIEW VERSE: 1 Samuel 20:4
4 So Jonathan said to David, "Whatever you yourself desire, I will do it for you."

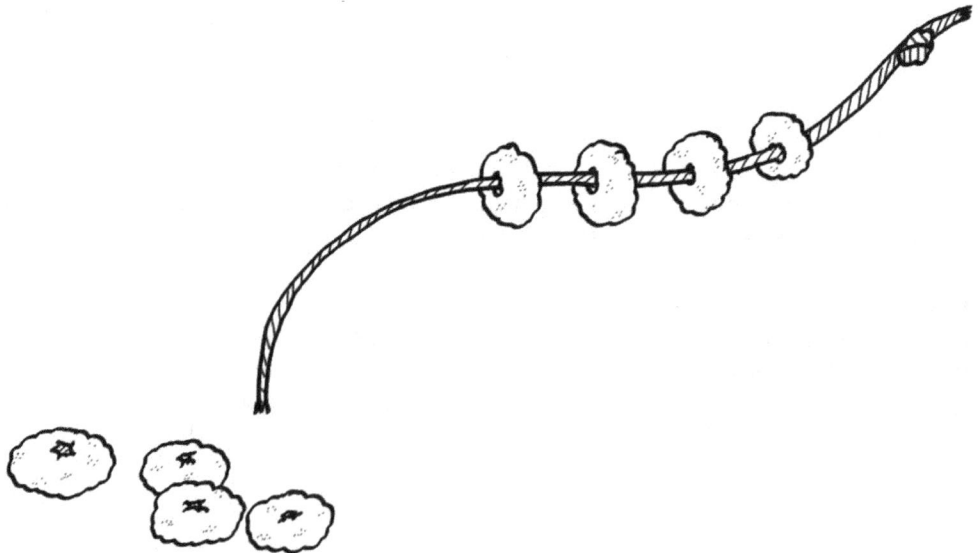

⑮ START A BAND

DISCUSSION:
Telling God how awesome He is through praise and worship is the greatest things we can do. Talk about how there are many ways to give praise.

SUPPLIES:
➢ Pots and Pans
➢ Spoons

ACTIVITY:
➢ Have the kids make up a song about how they feel about God
➢ They can use the pots and pans as instruments

REVIEW VERSE: Psalm 148:1-5
1 Praise the LORD! Praise the LORD from the heavens; Praise Him in the heights! 2 Praise Him, all His angels; Praise Him, all His hosts! 3 Praise Him, sun and moon; Praise Him, all you stars of light! 4 Praise Him, you heavens of heavens, and you waters above the heavens! 5 Let them praise the name of the LORD, For He commanded and they were created.

16

BUILD A TEMPLE

DISCUSSION:
Solomon went all out when he built this temple for the Lord. Talk to your kids about how we should go all out when we do things for God and for the people that we love, even if it's something we may not enjoy (like cleaning our rooms!)

SUPPLIES:
➤ Blocks or sand (at a local park)

ACTIVITY:
➤ Build a great temple, from either blocks or sand

REVIEW VERSE: 1 Kings 6:11-14
11 Then the word of the LORD came to Solomon, saying: 12 "Concerning this temple which you are building, if you walk in My statutes, execute My judgments, keep all My commandments, and walk in them, then I will perform My word with you, which I spoke to your father David. 13 And I will dwell among the children of Israel, and will not forsake My people Israel." 14 So Solomon built the temple and finished it.

(17)

MAKE DONUTS

DISCUSSION:
Explain that God fills us up with endless joy. He keeps giving us happiness and He never runs out.

SUPPLIES:
- Refrigerated biscuits
- Oil
- Cinnamon sugar or powder sugar

ACTIVITY:
- Put 4 tbsp oil into a skillet and let it heat up for two minutes
- Divide the biscuits into quarters, and place them into the oil
- Once they are cooked, let them cool minute before rolling them in sugar.

REVIEW VERSE: 1 Kings 17:12-14
12 So she said, "As the LORD your God lives, I do not have bread, only a handful of flour in a bin, and a little oil in a jar; and see, I am gathering a couple of sticks that I may go in and prepare it for myself and my son, that we may eat it, and die." 13 And Elijah said to her, "not fear; go and do as you have said, but make me a small cake from it first, and bring it to me; and afterward make some for yourself and your son. 14 For thus says the LORD God of Israel: 'The bin of flour shall not be used up, nor shall the of oil run dry, until the day the LORD sends rain on the earth.'"

⑱

REMEMBER ME BOX

DISCUSSION:
When we get busy in our lives, we sometimes forget our real purpose, which is to serve God. Talk about who God wants us to be and how He wants us to act.

SUPPLIES:
- An empty cardboard box
- Markers
- Paper

ACTIVITY:
- Write God's Mailbox on the cardboard box, and proceed to decorate it.
- Have the kids write letters to God about what they are going to do for God or how they are going to act, so that they can better resemble God's gracious ways.

REVIEW VERSE: 2 Kings 22:2
And he (Josiah) did right in the eyes of the Lord, and walked in all the ways of his father David; he did not turn aside to the right hand or to the left.

19

MAKE A MASK

DISCUSSION:
Discuss how to live a good life according to God's standards. What are standards? What are God's standards? Can we trust God always? The book of Daniel has some great answers. Talk about all the times that God has helped you in your life. Mention the story of Daniel and how God saved him from lions.

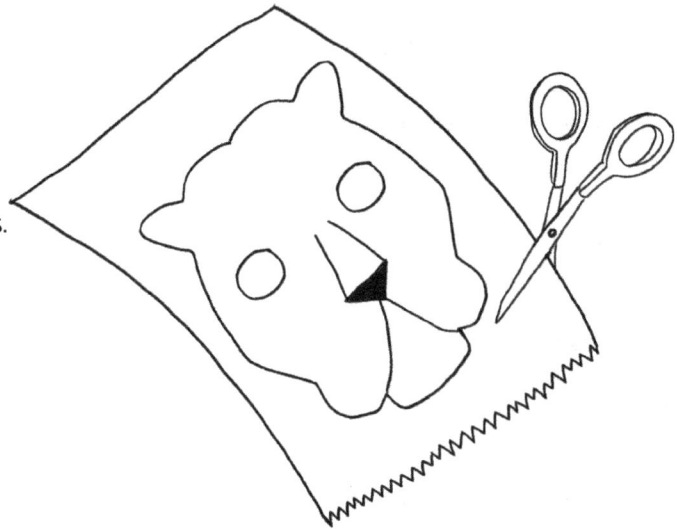

SUPPLIES:
➤ Brown paper grocery bags
➤ Markers or yellow construction paper
➤ Scissors
➤ Glue

ACTIVITY:
➤ Make a mask that resembles a lion
➤ Cut two holes for eyes in the brown paper bag
➤ You can pre-cut strips of yellow construction paper and glue them on to the paper bag as the mane or you can use the markers to color the mane.

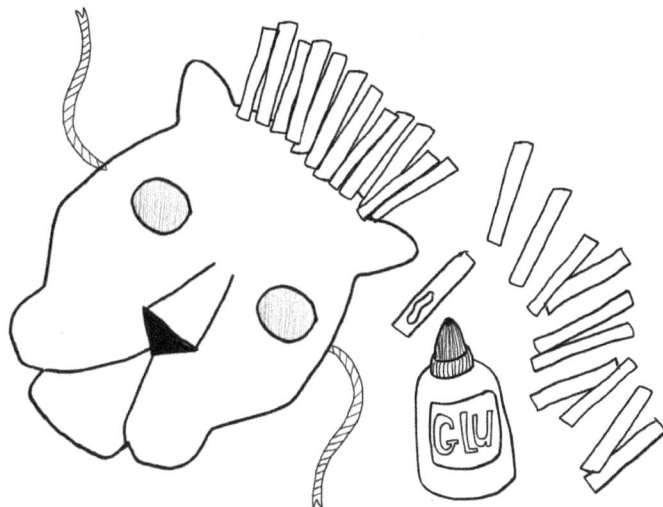

REVIEW VERSE: Daniel 6:11, 21-22
11 Then these men assembled and found Daniel praying and making supplication before his God. 20 And when he came to the den, he cried out with a lamenting voice to Daniel. The king spoke, saying to Daniel, "Daniel, servant of the living God, has your God, whom you serve continually, been able to deliver you from the lions?" 21 Then Daniel said to the king, "O king, live forever! 22 My God sent His angel and shut the lions' mouths, so that they have not hurt me, because I was found innocent before Him; and also, O king, I have done no wrong before you." not hurt me, because I was found innocent before Him; and also, O king, I have done no wrong before you."

(20)

WHALE HOUSE

DISCUSSION:

We all mess up. God is a God of second chances. Talk about Jonah and the Whale and how God gave Jonah a second chance. Tell your kids that it's okay to do something wrong, none of us are perfect and that it is good to grow from our failures. Let them know that God always wants us to try to do better and constantly improve as a person.

SUPPLIES:
➤ Large dark colored blanket or sheet
➤ Three bowls
➤ A can of tuna
➤ One package of jello
➤ A pack of crackers
➤ Two empty plastic bottles

ACTIVITY:
➤ Build a fort (the whale's stomach): this can be easily accomplished by hanging a large blanket of two chairs
➤ Fill one bowl with jello, one with tuna, and one with crackers.
➤ Sight- Have the child sit inside the fort and ask them how dark it must have been in the whale's stomach.
➤ Smell- Slide in the bowl of tuna for them to imagine how it must have smelled.
➤ Taste- Slide in a bowl of crackers, so they can taste the saltiness.
➤ Feel- Slide in the bowl of jello and tell them to feel how slimy it must have been.
➤ Hear- from outside the fort bang to bottles together to resemble the rumbling of the waves, and the burping of the whale, outside of the stomach.

REVIEW VERSE: Jonah 1:15,17. 2:1,10

15 So they picked up Jonah and threw him into the sea, and the sea ceased from its raging. 17 Now the LORD had prepared a great fish to swallow Jonah. And Jonah was in the belly of the fish three days and three nights. Jonah 2:1,10 Then Jonah prayed to the LORD his God from the fish's belly. 10 So the LORD spoke to the fish, and it vomited Jonah onto dry land.

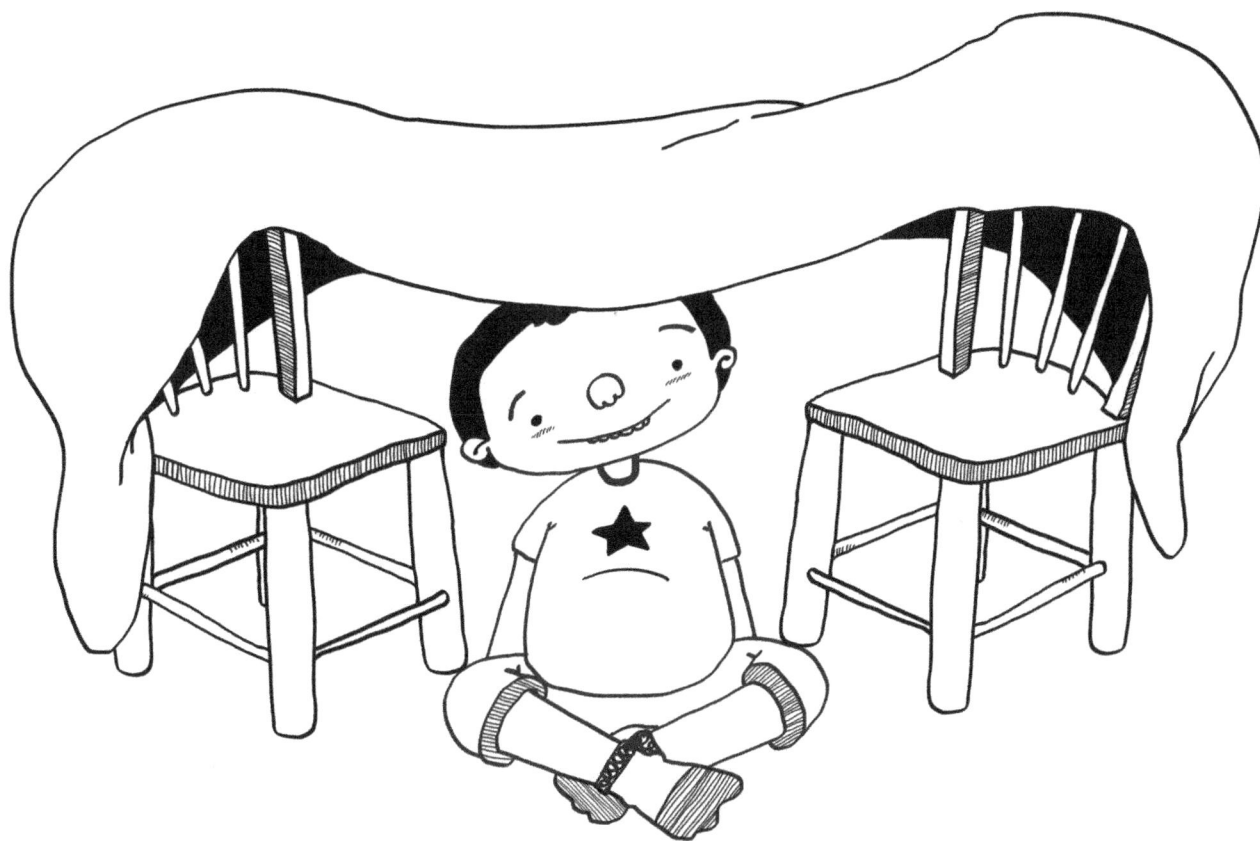

21

ANGEL ORNAMENT

DISCUSSION:
Talk about angels and about some of the miracles you have personally witnessed. Mention the miracle of Jesus – how he was born from the Virgin Mary and was fully God and fully Man.

SUPPLIES:
- 1/3 cup water
- ½ cup salt
- 1 cup flour
- Angel shaped cookie cutter
- String
- Paint or markers

ACTIVITY:
- Make an angel ornament by first mixing the water, salt and flour together.
- When mixture is stirred, it should be stuck together
- Remove the mixture and roll it out on to a cutting board
- Use the angel cookie cutter to create the shape of an angel
- Put an additional hole in the top of the angel for the string to go through
- Bake at 275 for one hour
- When cooled, decorate the angel with the markers or paint then put the string through the top hole, to hang it up.

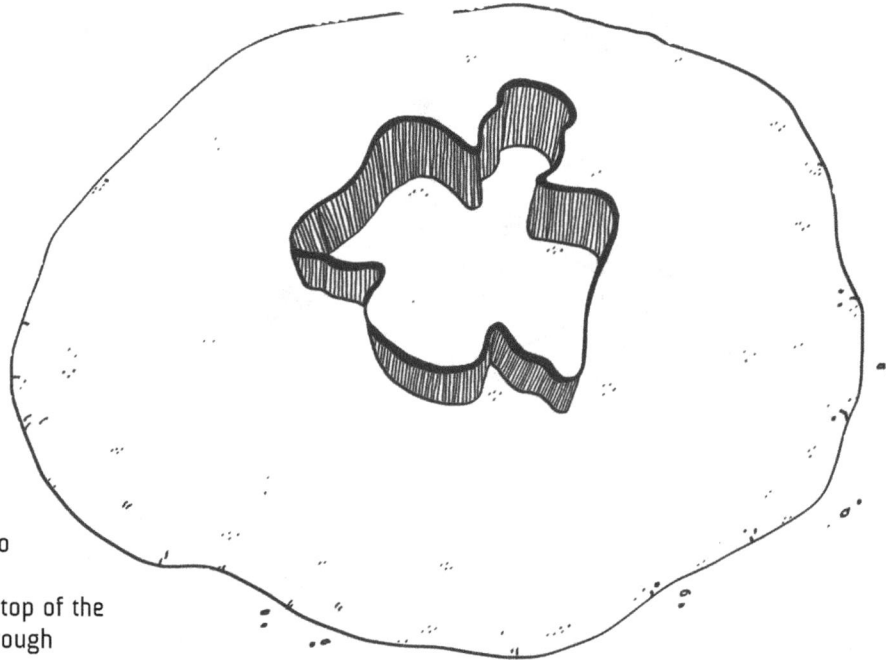

REVIEW VERSE: Luke 1:28-33
28 And having come in, the angel said to her, "Rejoice, highly favored one, the Lord is with you; blessed are you among women!" 29 But when she saw him, she was troubled at his saying, and considered what manner of greeting this was. 30 Then the angel said to her, "Do not be afraid, Mary, for you have found favor with God. 31 And behold, you will conceive in your womb and bring forth a Son, and shall call His name JESUS.

22

EDIBLE NATIVITY SCENE

DISCUSSION:

How awesome is it that the most powerful person in the universe, Jesus, was born in a stable for animals? Talk about how humble, but amazing Jesus is. Mention why we should be humble about ourselves, yet thankful and proud of what we do and accomplish. Talk about how you don't need a lot of things to be joyful and happy.

SUPPLIES:

➢ Plate
➢ Peanut Butter
➢ Graham Crackers
➢ Gummy Bears
➢ Shredded Mini Wheats
➢ Marshmallows
➢ Any other extra decorating goodies

ACTIVITY:

➢ Spread peanut butter over a plate
➢ Grab two graham crackers and tilt them, creating a triangle to resemble the stable. Use peanut butter as glue to stabilize them.
➢ Crush the shredded wheat cereal and spread it around the plate to resemble hay.
➢ Place marshmallows around the represent sheep
➢ Use the Gummy bears to resemble Mary, Joseph and Baby Jesus

REVIEW VERSE: Luke 2:4-7

4 Joseph also went up from Galilee, out of the city of Nazareth, into Judea, to the city of David, which is called Bethlehem, because he was of the house and lineage of David, 5 to be registered with Mary, his betrothed wife, who was with child. 6 So it was, that while they were there, the days were completed for her to be delivered. 7 And she brought forth her firstborn Son, and wrapped Him in swaddling cloths, and laid Him in a manger, because there was no room for them in the inn.

23

GIFT FOR JESUS

DISCUSSION:
Talk to your kids about all the gifts Jesus gives us. Ask them what they think Jesus would want from us. Let them know that it doesn't have to be a "thing," but maybe a "feeling" such as compassion and tell them that might be what Jesus would prefer.

SUPPLIES:
➢ Paper
➢ Crayons

ACTIVITY:
➢ Have everyone draw a picture of what gift they would give to Jesus if they had the opportunity.

REVIEW VERSE: Luke 2:26-32
26 And it had been revealed to him by the Holy Spirit that he would not see death before he had seen the Lord's Christ. 27 So he came by the Spirit into the temple. And when the parents brought in the Child Jesus, to do for Him according to the custom of the law, 28 he took Him up in his arms and blessed God and said: 29 "Lord, now You are letting Your servant depart in peace, according to Your word; 30 for my eyes have seen Your salvation 31 which You have prepared before the face of all peoples, 32 a light to bring revelation to the Gentiles, and the glory of Your people Israel."

MAKE A STAR ORNAMENT

DISCUSSION:
Nothing should stop us from worshipping Jesus. We can look up to the stars at night and see how awesome He is and how incredible our universe is. Talk about some things that can get in the way of remembering God's greatness and why we let that happen.

SUPPLIES:
➢ Popsicle sticks
➢ Markers
➢ Glue
➢ Stickers or glitter (Optional)

ACTIVITY:
➢ Use five popsicles and glue them together to create a star
➢ Wait ten minutes before you decorate.
➢ Use the markers and other craft supplies to decorate the star.

REVIEW VERSE: Matthew 2:7-11
7 Then Herod, when he had secretly called the wise men, determined from them what time the star appeared. 8 And he sent them to Bethlehem and said, "Go and search carefully for the young Child, and when you have found Him, bring back word to me, that I may come and worship Him also." 9 When they heard the king, they departed; and behold, the star which they had seen in the East went before them, till it came and stood over where the young Child was. 10 When they saw the star, they rejoiced with exceedingly great joy.

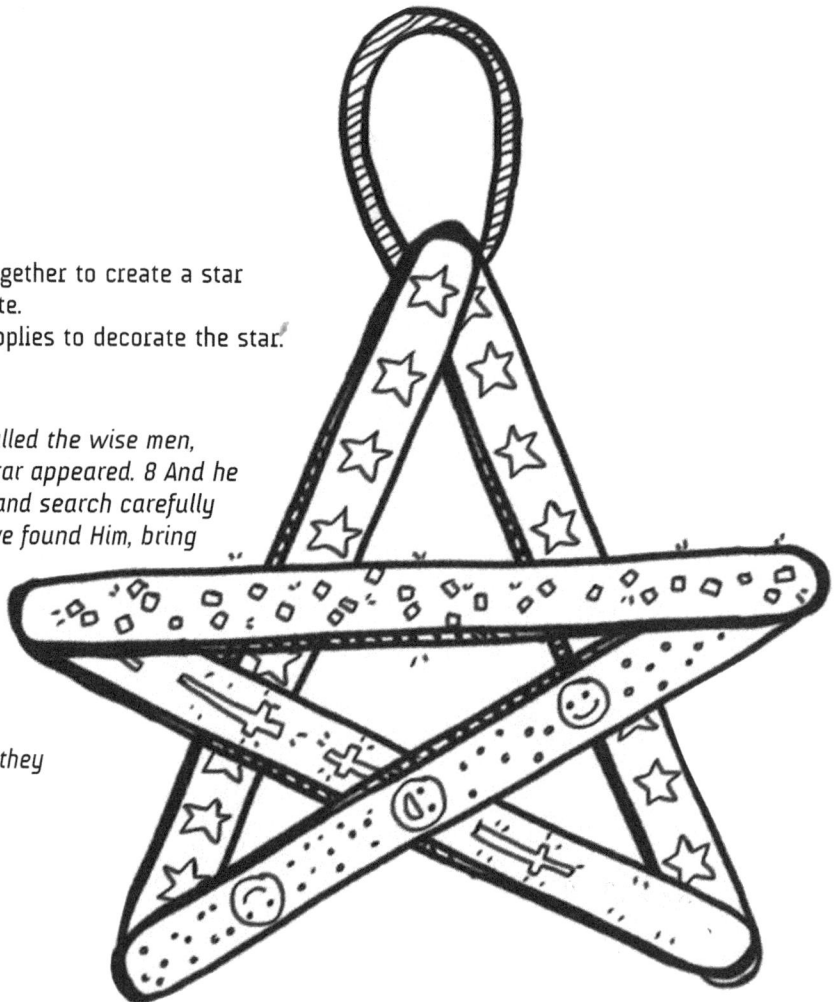

25

JESUS SAYS

DISCUSSION:
WWJD? What would Jesus do? We should be asking ourselves this everyday. Talk about Jesus's righteous actions and how the disciples followed his good lead.

SUPPLIES:
➤ At least two participants: one to lead, one to follow

ACTIVITY:
➤ Designate one person as the leader (Jesus) and everyone else as the followers (Disciples)
➤ The leader must say, "Jesus Says" followed by an action. For example, "Jesus says jump in the air." And the followers must jump.
➤ The leader can say "jump" and instead stand still, but no matter what, the followers must do as the leader says, not as the leader does. If a disciple gets confused and acts as the leader does rather than what the leader says, than they are out of this round.

REVIEW VERSE: Luke 5:4-6
4 When He had stopped speaking, He said to Simon, "Launch out into the deep and let down your nets for a catch." 5But Simon answered and said to Him, "Master, we have toiled all night and caught nothing; nevertheless at Your word I will let down the net." 6 And when they had done this, they caught a great number of fish, and their net was breaking.

26

SPREAD THE WEALTH

DISCUSSION:
Talk about how God promises to take care of us even better than the birds and the flowers. He loves us so much! Talk about how we still must honor the animals though because God presents us with them to keep us company and help fill the world. Talk about how we can help God look after the animals.

SUPPLIES:
➢ Bag of bread
➢ Ducks and/or fish

ACTIVITY:
➢ Go to a local lake or river.
➢ While enjoying the nature, feed the fish and birds by throwing your bread into the water.

REVIEW VERSE: Matthew 6:31-34
31 "Therefore do not worry, saying, 'What shall we eat?' or 'What shall we drink?' or 'What shall we wear?' 32 For after all these things the Gentiles seek. For your heavenly Father knows that you need all these things. 33 But seek first the kingdom of God and His righteousness, and all these things shall be added to you. 34 Therefore do not worry about tomorrow, for tomorrow will worry about its own things. Sufficient for the day is its own trouble.

㉗

GROW A PLANT

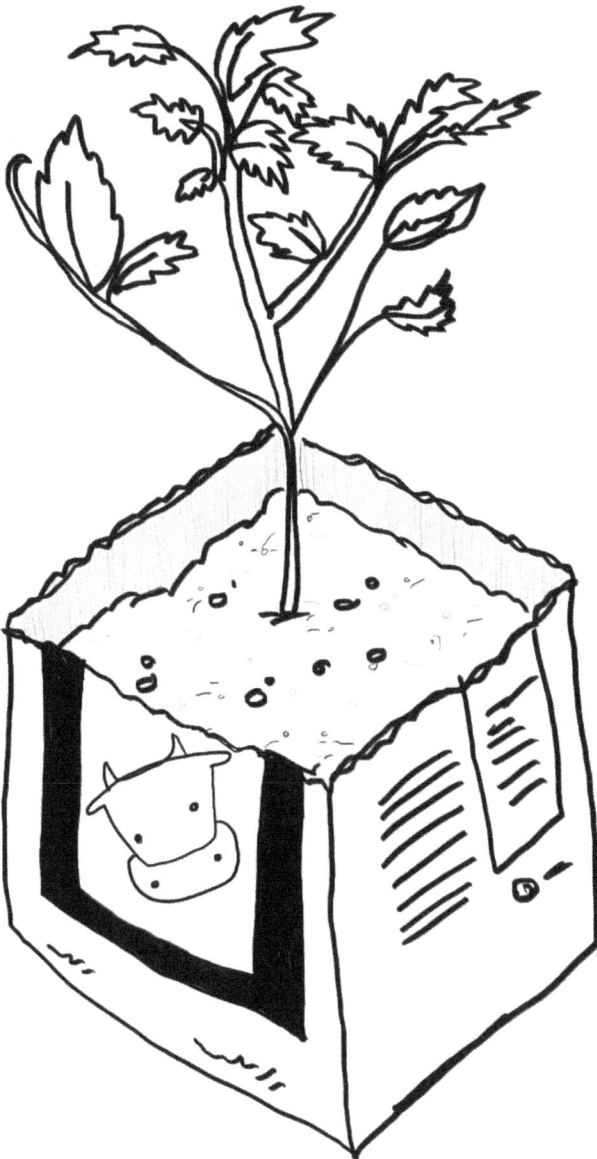

DISCUSSION:
It's hard to imagine that such a small seed can turn into a beautiful plant. Talk about all the small gifts that God has given to us. Not a home or a beautiful city, but small things, like a good sense of smell, a funny goldfish, your Mom's beautiful hair, etc.

SUPPLIES:
➢ Half of a milk carton
➢ Dirt
➢ Seed for plant of choice

ACTIVITY:
➢ Line the bottom of the milk carton with dirt
➢ Place the seed in the dirt, then proceed to cover it over with more dirt
➢ Watch how the seed grows over time.

REVIEW VERSE: Matthew 13:31,32
31 Another parable He put forth to them, saying: "The kingdom of heaven is like a mustard seed, which a man took and sowed in his field, 32 which indeed is the least of all the seeds; but when it is grown it is greater than the herbs and becomes a tree, so that the birds of the air come and nest in its branches."

28

TREASURE HUNT

DISCUSSION:
A friendship with Jesus is the greatest treasure of all. Talk about all the treasures Jesus has blessed you with. These can be big and weird, or small and special!

SUPPLIES:
- Gold spray paint
- Permanent black marker
- Pile of medium sized rocks
- Big area to play

ACTIVITY:
- Spray paint all of the rocks gold, to resemble treasure.
- Allow a sufficient amount of time for the rocks to completely dry.
- On the rock, have the kids use permanent markers to write all the treasures that Jesus has given them.
- Then go hide the treasure throughout the designated area
- On the parents cue, have the kids search the area for all the treasures.

REVIEW VERSE: Matthew 13:44-46
44 *"Again, the kingdom of heaven is like treasure hidden in a field, which a man found and hid; and for joy over it he goes and sells all that he has and buys that field. 45 "Again, the kingdom of heaven is like a merchant seeking beautiful pearls, 46 who, when he had found one pearl of great price, went and sold all that he had and bought it."*

29

THE GOOD SAMARITANS

DISCUSSION:
Jesus is very kind. We should be too. Talk to your kids about giving back to others in your community and recognizing when others are in need. Tell them how good it feels to help someone else out.

SUPPLIES:
➢ Paper
➢ Markers

ACTIVITY:
➢ Write a letter to someone you know that you want to reach out to. Maybe you know someone who is sick or sad. Maybe someone once helped you in a time of need and you want to thank them for doing so.

REVIEW VERSE: Luke 10:30-37
30 Then Jesus answered and said: "A certain man went down from Jerusalem to Jericho, and fell among thieves, who stripped him of his clothing, wounded him, and departed, leaving him half dead. 31 Now by chance a certain priest came down that road. And when he saw him, he passed by on the other side. 32 Likewise a Levite, when he arrived at the place, came and looked, and passed by on the other side. 33 But a certain Samaritan, as he journeyed, came where he was. And when he saw him, he had compassion. 34 So he went to him and bandaged his wounds, pouring on oil and wine; and he set him on his own animal, brought him to an inn, and took care of him.

(30)

THE QUEST

DISCUSSION:
Talk about how passionate Jesus is about finding us. Explain that Jesus is constantly in search of us, because He wants all of us to be with him one day again.

SUPPLIES:
- Paper
- Writing utensil
- Chocolate gold coins (any variation of candy/treat will do)

ACTIVITY:
- The parent should draw a map for the children to follow.
- Have the map lead them to different locations throughout the designated playing area.
- At these locations, have a gold coin waiting for them.
- The final location should have a pile of gold coins
- Have the kids gather all the coins they found and split them equally among each other.

REVIEW VERSE: Luke 15:8-10
8 "Or what woman, having ten silver coins, if she loses one coin, does not light a lamp, sweep the house, and search carefully until she finds it? 9And when she has found it, she calls her friends and neighbors together, saying, 'Rejoice with me, for I have found the piece which I lost!' 10 Likewise, I say to you, there is joy in the presence of the angels of God over one sinner who repents."

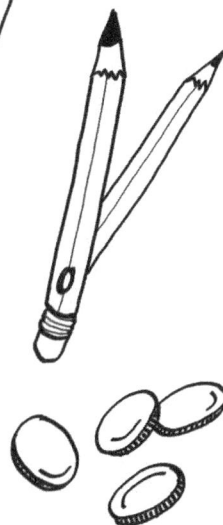

BLIND OBSTACLES

DISCUSSION:
Discuss the blind man, Bartimaeus, and how Jesus helped him have sight. Although our powers are not as great as Jesus, we too can help others.

SUPPLIES:
➢ A bandana or piece of cloth.
➢ Plastic cones (often used on athletic fields)

ACTIVITY:
➢ Blind one child by tying the bandana around his eyes
➢ Set up an obstacle course
➢ Have another child guide him through the obstacle course just by voice.

REVIEW VERSE: Mark 10:46-52
46 Now they came to Jericho. As He went out of Jericho with His disciples and a great multitude, blind Bartimaeus, the son of Timaeus, sat by the road begging. 47 And when he heard that it was Jesus of Nazareth, he began to cry out and say, "Jesus, Son of David, have mercy on me!" 48 Then many warned him to be quiet; but he cried out all the more, "Son of David, have mercy on me!" 49 So Jesus stood still and commanded him to be called. Then they called the blind man, saying to him, "Be of good cheer. Rise, He is calling you." 50 And throwing aside his garment, he rose and came to Jesus. 51 So Jesus answered and said to him, "What do you want Me to do for you?" The blind man said to Him, "Rabboni, that I may receive my sight." 52 Then Jesus said to him, "Go your way; your faith has made you well." And immediately he received his sight and followed Jesus on the road.

③② BREAKING BREAD

DISCUSSION:
Explain why communion is important. Explain that the bread broken at communion is a representation of how Jesus is the bread of life. Explain that the wine symbolizes the blood that Jesus shed, so that our sins will be forgiven. Mention the Last Supper and all of the people that joined Jesus in that meal.

SUPPLIES:
➢ Paper
➢ Crayons

ACTIVITY:
➢ Have each child draw a picture of them breaking bread with the people that they would most enjoy having dinner with.

REVIEW VERSE: Matthew 26:26-30
26 And as they were eating, Jesus took bread, blessed and broke it, and gave it to the disciples and said, "Take, eat; this is My body." 27 Then He took the cup, and gave thanks, and gave it to them, saying, "Drink from it, all of you. 28 For this is My blood of the new covenant, which is shed for many for the remission of sins. 29 But I say to you, I will not drink of this fruit of the vine from now on until that day when I drink it new with you in My Father's kingdom." 30 And when they had sung a hymn, they went out to the Mount of Olives.

(33) KEEPSAKE

DISCUSSION:
Talk about the significance of the cross. Explain how it is a constant reminder of Jesus' sacrifice.

SUPPLIES:
➢ Popsicle stick
➢ Markers
➢ Tape
➢ String
➢ Glue

ACTIVITY:
➢ Glue two popsicle sticks together to create a cross or "t" shape.
➢ Have the kids decorate their crosses
➢ Tape a string to the back of the cross, so that the kids can hang their cross in a special place.

REVIEW VERSE: John 19:17-42
17 And He, bearing His cross, went out to a place called the Place of a Skull, which is called in Hebrew, Golgotha, 18 where they crucified Him, and two others with Him, one on either side, and Jesus in the center. 19 Now Pilate wrote a title and put it on the cross. And the writing was: JESUS OF NAZARETH, THE KING OF THE JEWS.

㉞ RESSURECTION COOKIES

DISCUSSION:
Jesus' death on the cross is a tragic and heart wrenching story. However, Jesus' strength and power does not stop there. He rises, to prove he is very much alive and out to save us.

SUPPLIES:
➢ Mixing bowl
➢ 1 cup of whole pecans
➢ 1 tsp vinegar
➢ 3 egg whites
➢ Pinch of salt
➢ 1 cup of sugar
➢ Zip-lock baggie
➢ Piece of tape

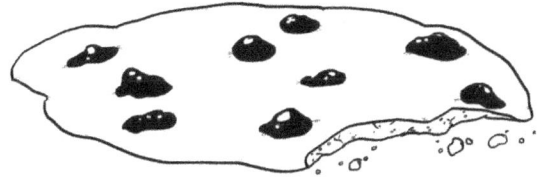

ACTIVITY:
➢ Preheat oven to 300 degrees
➢ Put pecans in the baggie. Beat them to represent how Jesus was beaten by the Roman soldiers. John 19:1-3
➢ Smell the vinegar. Put it in the mixing bowl. Jesus was offered this to drink on the cross. John 19:28-30
➢ Add egg whites to the bowl. Eggs represent life. Jesus gave His life to give us eternal life. John 10:10-11
➢ Add the salt. Let each child taste a little salt. It represents the tears He shed in Gethsemane. Matthew 26:36-46
➢ Add 1 cup of sugar. Let child taste grains of sugar. The sweetest part of this story is that He died, because He loves us so much. John 3:16
➢ Adult: beat with a mixer until stiff peaks form. The white is for the purity and cleanliness we have when we ask Jesus to forgive us our sins. Isaiah 1:18

➢ Fold in the broken nuts. Put wax paper on a cookie sheet. Drop mounds onto wax paper to represent the rocky tomb for Jesus. Matt. 27:57-60
➢ Put cookie sheet in the oven. Turn the oven off. Give each child tape to seal the oven shut (wear oven mitts please). The tomb was sealed shut Matthew 27:65-66
➢ Go to bed. It is sad to leave the cookies. The disciples were sad to leave Jesus. John 16:20, 22
➢ On the first Easter everyone was surprised that the tomb was empty. Take a bite of the cookie. They are empty inside just like the tomb. HE IS RISEN! Matt. 28:1-9

(35)

FOLLOW THE LIGHT

DISCUSSION:
Know that Jesus can bring us from bad to good, or lead us from the dark to the light.

SUPPLIES:
➢ Flashlights
➢ Big playing area

ACTIVITY:
➢ One person starts as the "Seeker," (Jesus)
➢ All others will pretend to be Saul and hide from Jesus
➢ After the Seeker counts to 30, he of she must find the ones hiding and shine the flashlight on them.
➢ Once you are caught, you "go into the light" and become a seeker.
➢ Play until everyone is found.

REVIEW VERSE: Acts 9:1-6,
1 Then Saul, still breathing threats and murder against the disciples of the Lord, went to the high priest 2 and asked letters from him to the synagogues of Damascus, so that if he found any who were of the Way, whether men or women, he might bring them bound to Jerusalem. 3 As he journeyed he came near Damascus, and suddenly a light shone around him from heaven. 4 Then he fell to the ground, and heard a voice saying to him, "Saul, Saul, why are you persecuting Me?" 5 And he said, "Who are You, Lord?" Then the Lord said, "I am Jesus, whom you are persecuting. It is hard for you to kick against the goads." 6 So he, trembling and astonished, said, "Lord, what do You want me to do?" Then the Lord said to him, "Arise and go into the city, and you will be told what you must do."

36

COLOR HEAVEN

DISCUSSION:
Heaven is going to be beautiful. We must receive God's free gift, Jesus, as our very own to be with Him forever.

SUPPLIES:
➢ Paper
➢ Crayons
➢ Yellow water-color paint

ACTIVITY:
➢ Have each child use the crayons to draw a picture of how they imagine Heaven will look
➢ Once their pictures are complete, paint over it with yellow water color paint, to show the gold of Heaven

REVIEW VERSE: Revelation 21:2
Then I John saw the Holy City, New Jerusalem coming down out of heaven from God prepared as a bride adorned for her husband.

PART TWO

Everyday ways to incorporate the Bible

❶

CONFIDENCE COMES WITH COMPLIMENTS

We all make mistakes, but the important thing is that we are constantly trying to improve ourselves. God smiles when we give with a good attitude and when we give more than what is asked for. Even when your kids do something small, let them know you are proud of them.

RELATABLE VERSE: Genesis 24: 18-19
18 So she said, "Drink, my lord." Then she quickly let her pitcher down to her hand, and gave him a drink. 19 And when she had finished giving him a drink, she said, "I will draw water for your camels also, until they have finished drinking."

2

BLESSING FOR DESSERT

Before celebrating the completion of another day over a delicious dessert, say a blessing.

RELATABLE VERSE: Genesis 27: 26-29
26 Then his father Isaac said to him, "Come near now and kiss me, my son." 27 And he came near and kissed him; and he smelled the smell of his clothing, and blessed him and said "Surely, the smell of my son is like the smell of a field which the LORD has blessed. 28 Therefore may God give you of the dew of heaven, of the fatness of the earth, and plenty of grain and wine.

3

HAVE FAITH

When your children are facing something new or something they are unsure of, tell them to follow their heart. Talk about how God is with them always and to have faith. Remind them of the story of Moses, the strength of his mother, and what he became.

RELATABLE VERSE: Exodus 2: 1-3,10

2 So the woman conceived and bore a son. And when she saw that he was a beautiful child, she hid him three months. 3 But when she could no longer hide him, she took an ark of bulrushes for him, daubed it with asphalt and pitch, put the child in it, and laid it in the reeds by the river's bank. 10 And the child grew, and she brought him to Pharaoh's daughter, and he became her son. So she called his name Moses, saying, "because I drew him out of the water".

4

NOTICE THE GOOD

It's easy to look at the bad, but God says we are fearfully and wonderfully made. When you and your family are walking around, make note of these good things. If you see someone doing something nice then point it out to your kids.

RELATABLE VERSE: Numbers 13:19-20
19 whether the land they dwell in is good or bad; whether the cities they inhabit are like camps or strongholds; 20 whether the land is rich or poor; and whether there are forests there or not. Be of good courage. And bring some of the fruit of the land."

Nice Things I Pointed Out to People This Week

_____

_____

_____

_____

_____

_____

_____

_____

_____

_____

_____

_____

_____

_____

_____

5

GIVE AND TAKE

Presents are often given to show someone how much they are loved or cared about. Next time Christmas or a child's birthday comes around, have them write down what they want, but talk to them about why they want these gifts. Ask them how these gifts will help them live the life that Jesus intended.

RELATABLE VERSE: 1 Samuel 1:27, 28

27 For this child I prayed, and the LORD has granted me my petition which I asked of Him. 28 Therefore I also have lent him to the LORD; as long as he lives he shall be lent to the LORD." So they worshiped the LORD there.

COOL GIFT LIST FOR HELPING OTHERS

6

TRAVEL IN FAITH

It's a great thing to want God's power in your life. While driving or pulling your kids in a wagon, take the opportunity to share the story of Elisha and how God helped him.

RELATABLE VERSE: 2 Kings 6:16-17
16 So he answered, "Do not fear, for those who are with us are more than those who are with them." 17 And Elisha prayed, and said, "LORD, I pray, open his eyes that he may see." Then the LORD opened the eyes of the young man, and he saw. And behold, the mountain was full of horses and chariots of fire all around Elisha.

How Did God Help Elisha?

_____

_____

_____

_____

_____

_____

_____

_____

_____

_____

_____

_____

_____

_____

_____

_____

_____

7

TABLE TALK

It's never a bad time to talk about God. Mention Him even when times are bad or when it seems hard to follow in His commands. Obey God and watch what He does for you.

RELATABLE VERSE: Daniel 3:17
17 If that is the case, our God whom we serve is able to deliver us from the burning fiery furnace, and He will deliver us from your hand, O king.

WHAT HAS GOD DONE FOR US THIS MONTH?

_____

_____

_____

_____

_____

_____

_____

_____

_____

_____

_____

_____

_____

_____

8

GARDENING TALK

Taking advantage of nature should always be a part of your day. Plant a garden, watch it grow, have your family get involved in it. While gardening, you can discuss how Jesus told a story about how a "sower went out to sow," and even though so many failed, there were some that didn't.

RELATABLE VERSE: Matthew 13: 8
8 But others fell on good ground and yielded a crop: some a hundredfold, some sixty, some thirty.

9

GO FISHING

Fishing is great for family time and some quality talk about life. Mention Jesus and how one day He will look at everyone's hearts and separate the good (forgiven) from the bad (unrepentant).

RELATABLE VERSE: Matthew 13:47-51
49 So it will be at the end of the age. The angels will come forth, separate the wicked from among the just,

10

SWIM LESSONS

While hanging out in the pool on a hot summer day, why not bring up Jesus? He did walk on water. Talk about all the other amazing things He did.

RELATABLE VERSE: Matthew 14:26-29
26 And when the disciples saw Him walking on the sea, they were troubled, saying, "It is a ghost!" And they cried out for fear. 27 But immediately Jesus spoke to them, saying, "Be of good cheer! It is I; do not be afraid." 28 And Peter answered Him and said, "Lord, if it is You, command me to come to You on the water." 29 So He said, "Come." And when Peter had come down out of the boat, he walked on the water to go to Jesus.

11

ALONE TIME

Teach you kids to listen to the quiet voice in their heart. Tell them to make an effort to spend at least five minutes alone with God a day. Tell them to talk to Him, share their feelings, thoughts, and questions. God wants to have a special relationship with each of us.

RELATABLE VERSE: Luke 10: 39-42
39 And she had a sister called Mary, who also sat at Jesus' feet and heard His word. 40 But Martha was distracted with much serving, and she approached Him and said, "Lord, do You not care that my sister has left me to serve alone? Therefore tell her to help me." 41 And Jesus answered and said to her, "Martha, Martha, you are worried and troubled about many things. 42 But one thing is needed, and Mary has chosen that good part, which will not be taken away from her."

12

FOR THE PARENTS

Children are a gift from the Lord! Sometimes your kids might bug you, cramp your style, or wear you out. It's okay! Ask Jesus for help. Ask Him for His eyes to see them the way He does. Ask the Lord for the strength to treasure their innocence, wonderment, free spirits, sweet and tender moments, their beauty, and their eagerness to learn new things.

RELATABLE VERSE: PS 127:3. Luke 18:15-17
3 Behold, children are a heritage from the LORD, The fruit of the womb is a reward.

13

CLIMBING TREES

If your kids are just hanging out, maybe climbing trees to pass the time, tell them the story of Zaccheus. Ask your kids what they would do to help Jesus.

RELATABLE VERSE: Luke 19:4-5
4 So he ran ahead and climbed up into a sycamore tree to see Him, for He was going to pass that way. 5 And when Jesus came to the place, He looked up and saw him, and said to him, "Zacchaeus, make haste and come down, for today I must stay at your house."

14

BLOWING BUBBLES

Blowing bubbles is a cheap and fun past time. See if your children can catch the bubbles without popping them. Throw in a little bible talk. Unlike the temporary bubbles, God never sleeps or slumbers. He is always listening and working on our hearts and our lives. God never leaves us.

RELATABLE VERSE: John 5:6-9

6 When Jesus saw him lying there, and knew that he already had been in that condition a long time, He said to him, "Do you want to be made well?"7 The sick man answered Him, "Sir, I have no man to put me into the pool when the water is stirred up; but while I am coming, another steps down before me." 8 Jesus said to him, "Rise, take up your bed and walk." 9 And immediately the man was made well, took up his bed, and walked. And that day was the Sabbath.

15

FOOT RUBS

We should always be giving the best of our time and talents—not leftovers. Share a foot massage, or a toy, but give to your loved ones the best that you can. Jesus is happy when we give our best.

RELATABLE VERSE: John 12: 3
3 Then Mary took a pound of very costly oil of spikenard, anointed the feet of Jesus, and wiped His feet with her hair. And the house was filled with the fragrance of the oil.

16

CAMPING AND SPOTTING FOOD

Have a camp out, make S'mores, spend time thanking God for all of the things you have and all the things you are able to do. Try and name all the things in the wild that can be eaten that God gave us, including the types of fish. Bring a nature book and see if you can get to 100.

RELATABLE VERSE: John 21:5-6
5 Then Jesus said to them, "Children, have you any food?" They answered Him, "No." 6 And He said to them, "Cast the net on the right side of the boat, and you will find some." So they cast, and now they were not able to draw it in because of the multitude of fish.

LIST OF THINGS WE SAW

_____

_____

_____

_____

_____

_____

_____

_____

_____

_____

_____

_____

_____

_____

_____

17

CLOUD WATCHING

While using your imagination to name cloud airplanes or cloud dinosaurs, talk about how it must have looked when Jesus was ascending to Heaven.

RELATABLE VERSE: Acts 1: 9-10
9 Now when He had spoken these things, while they watched, He was taken up, and a cloud received Him out of their sight. 10 And while they looked steadfastly toward heaven as He went up, behold, two men stood by them in white apparel.

What We Saw in the Clouds

_____

_____

_____

_____

_____

_____

_____

_____

_____

_____

_____

_____

_____

_____

_____

www.ingramcontent.com/pod-product-compliance
Lightning Source LLC
Chambersburg PA
CBHW081134090426
42737CB00018B/3346